```
I0160703
```

Dedicated to all the victims around the world whose death was at the hand of another human being. We all need to do better.

All Black Lives Matter.
Love is Love.
My body, my choice.
Stop Asian Hate.
Peace not War.

Love + Light
-G.TW + C.A.T

I CAN'T BREATHE

Gioya Tuma-Waku
Chaise Angelo Tait

More information at www.perfectlyimperfectent.com

G.TW poems edited by Patricia Kass.
ISBN: 978-1-7347659-1-5

Dedicated to all the victims around the world whose death was caused by another human being.
We need to do better.

All Black Lives Matter.
Love is Love.
My body, My choice.
Stop Asian Hate.
Peace not War.

Love + Light
- G.TW + C.A.T.

CONTENTS

RISE

Welcome home
But also welcome to paradise
A warm welcome from your mother's light
To create stars is a divine feminine birthright
I came here in a space suit designed by her beauty
To get through this life with love as my only duty
I am here to observe the golden age of my people
Great Kings will rise to protect a new love that is
gentle
A love that is sacred and a love that stands true
One that brings the great mother back into crystal
clear view
A 20/20 view
With 20/21 advantage
She is my legend
She is my anthem
I represent the black woman
And I do it with passion
-C.A.T.

TO BE AND BE BORN BLACK

To be black in this city is to live with the industry's blurred perception of me.

To be black in this city is not knowing how to show up and just be.

Our sun kissed skin envied as you periodically sit for hours in the sun.

The same skin the very reason we get raped, lynched, and shot.

As we struggle for jobs and auditions while the Oscars stay so white.

To be qualified or overqualified and still feel invisible in the light.

To be black in this state is to dance with restraint no matter the season.

To be black in this state is to be hated for no apparent reason.

Our spirits crying on the souls of our ancestors.

Blood tears stream while your words burn like chemotherapy.

Walking calmly down the street while you fearfully cross to the other side.

The most liberal state includes LAPD leading with the most police brutality crimes.

To be black in this country is to experience unrequited love and feel 'unpretty.'
To be black in this country is to constantly tremble in our authenticity.
Wanting to be free but our souls can never settle.
Crying 'I CAN'T BREATHE' as we choke from the pressure.
Our art, music and creativity rejoiced and appropriated.
While taking a knee causes more anger than police kneeing us until we're debilitated.

To be black on this continent is to cry for an unborn baby's future.
To be black on this continent is constantly weeping and questioning how to feature.
Never offered a seat at the table in the room where decisions happen.
Always unheard and misunderstood until we take arms.
Our ancestors built these countries under severe duress, so hellish.
While as women we are the subject of a never-ending fetish.

To be black on this earth is to be born with the light taken from your eyes.
To be black on this earth is to be surrounded by generational lies.
No silver spoon to help us get ahead.

Taking our first steps with a target on our backs.

Cries of racism and injustice falling on deaf ears.

Fighting for what our ancestors died for, as if they were our peers.

To be black on this planet is to be dehumanised and plus -

To be black on this planet is to continuously rise above the system that chokes us.

The battlefield is never on our own grounds.

Always a guest on their home court advantage.

Complying out of fear for our lives is the basic notion.

Black men unable to be vulnerable or show emotion.

To be black in this world is to never be at peace with what's on a history book's page.

To be black in this world is to be born filled with so much rage.

To live through the toughest of struggles.

Informed by a few shades of colour.

Melanin shading us from the sun.

While we crumble at the hands of mankind's gun.

To be black is feeling fat 'cos we got hips.

To be black is feeling ugly 'cos our hair nappy.

To be black is feeling dirty 'cos our skin dark.

To be black is feeling insecure 'cos we speak in slang.

To be born black is to fear a higher rate of death at childbirth.

To be born black is to panic for our lives at the thought of being pulled over.

To be born black is to be too scared to leave the house.

To be born black is to be too frightened to sleep in our own bed.

To be born black is to be born 700m behind an 800m race,
Sprinting for our lives but we can never win or catch their pace.

To be born black is to constantly adjust my movement in society,
To make sure that other races are not filled with any anxiety.

To be born black is to let Martin stay asleep,
Because in this reality his dreams feel so unattainable that he would just weep.

To be born black is feeling society hate you so much.
You contemplate doing what Michael did,
Almost but not quite.

No matter where you are in the world,
To be and be born black,
Is a death sentence,
and that's a fact.
-G.TW

SHINE ON ALL OF THEM

When I surround myself with beautiful black women
I call it a full moon
Taurus is the season and she has come to soothe all
her children's wounds
For we are long overdue
And our pride shows it too
I lay down my ego
And embrace the love shining through
The one I always knew was true
-C.A.T.

We just want to be seen
Really seen
For more than just the shade of our skin
Or the gender of our sex
Much less the sex of our partner (s)
-G.TW

GROWING

I crushed you into orange
As you melted into the blue
Over crystal green waters
My soul finally found you
Sitting in silence
Watching love crash the shore
Conquering all my hate
As each one finds the seafloor
For I am complete
For I have become much more
-C.A.T.

COMPETITION

I am not in competition
    Not with any female or male
    I move in love and light only
    If you want me
    Then I'm yours for free
    If you want her
    I'll step aside gladly
    I will not be scared off.
    But I won't stick around,
    Waiting for naïveté,
    To set me aside,
    For me to see what's really going on.
    I love you too much to make you choose
    I love me too much to welcome the blues
    -G.TW

BREAKTHROUGH

Things are so peaceful here
My mind expands and my thoughts are clear
I find voices in the wind that sing along with our
grins
They say we are special and have all the light we
need
But it starts with love
Or something as simple as a hug
It starts with calling someone you thought of
Saying something you felt but never was bold enough
to say
Except today has come and that feeling has passed
away
We are honest
We are pure
We are free
We create love with soft voices and rhythmic
melodies
Come bask in this happiness with me
Follow the seasons and you will enjoy limitless
company
-C.A.T.

There's a freedom that exists
    When you drop the layers
    Restraint bound by chains
    Stand in your truth
    Allow the sun to shine
    Warm your inner child
    Free your creative soul
    Feed your spiritual animal
    Turn away from the forbidden fruit
    Relish the garden of purity
    -G.TW

Little astronaut in your little space suit,
Don't forget mamma loves you.
-C.A.T.

#CHALLENGEACCEPTED

Women supporting women
  Accepting that black and white challenge
  Highlighting that femicide
  Turkey, South Africa, London
  Our female lives matter
  More than just your egg donor
  Or your pleasure holder
  Kidnapped, raped and brutally murdered
  Equal value; unequal pay
  There is more to us than your black and white
  More than just being your wife.
  We are the colour brightening up your life
  But all you see is red
  Red when you handle us aggressively
  Red when you take us mercilessly
  Red when you take our lives with your hands
  Playing God with our bodies and lives
  While I'm out here birthing your ass
  Do you see her face when you lift up her skirt?
  Or as she's continuously yelling no?
  Or even when she's not conscious enough to
consent?
  Is that what it means to be a real man?

What did your mama say when she raised you?
What do you fear walking your sister to safety?
You can't wait to buy your mama a place
But your actions would wipe the smile off her face.

-G.TW

THE OASIS

Don't let anyone tell you you're not real. Your hips, your curves, your intelligent appeal. You put words together and made them feel real. Black women treat me like royalty because I love them for real.

I relax my joints and stretch my arms out across the golden plains. My heart is the center of your indigo purple rain. It pours and it gives with no shame. Unattached to anything that tries to give love a bad name. You make me pure and something more than just a title or last name.

I've traveled a long way but I bring fresh water from the mountains. I bring myself to peace by restoring your beautiful fountain. I am whole, I am home, I am at the gathering place. I'm quite sure I finally found the place.

Fill your cups with joy. Clear skies show signs that ancestors jump for joy. Do it now while you're here in the moment.

You finally found peace, therefore your love is no longer stolen.

-C.A.T.

I kept looking outside of myself,
Hoping to find you there.
When I finally looked inside my heart,
I found that you had been there all along.
-G.TW

PEECHZ

She came to me in my dreams,
So I put her to my mouth like peach cobbler and ice
cream.
See now I'm a feign, for just that one Queen.
She has many forms, and she carries many things,
But my favorite happens to be peach cobbler and ice
cream.
Everyday I make her whatever I want.
My dough, my cinnamon, my yellow cling peach.
I eat every spoonful of you and melt you down with
my tongue and dimpled cheeks.
A whole pan of you for myself is what I seek.
Lay back and let the student teach.
This is what I like to call my favorite peach.
-C.A.T.

CONNECT

Our souls connect
    We talk music
    We watch movies
    And share tv shows.
    That first day
    An instant connection.
    Never could I believe
    You could walk into my life,
    And see my soul.
    I'm in big trouble,
    Cos our bodies connected.
    That shit was deep man
    Loving on me like you in love
    Kissing on me like I'm a temple
    Caring for me
    Protective over me
    And it's been two days
    Only two days since we met
    But our souls connect
    -G.TW

STRANGER THINGS

Found a little peace so I ran with it,
I took it to my ancestors and sat in it,
I put my hands behind my head and laid with it,
And I soon came to find out, there's more of it.
Plenty more,
Every store sells a fake but at home is where she
grows pure.
Away from distractions,
And away from the main attractions,
Time and space become nothing once love is our only
satisfaction.
-C.A.T.

You've never had such a hard time leaving a conversation. Wow. Neither have I. Your smile lights up your whole face and my whole body is filled with joy. Howzit you get me so fast? Howzit you see past the hurt and pain and come and upend my world? I never needed a man to show me my worth, but you treasured my core and found me worthy. Thanks for the reminder. Worthy of myself and finally awakening the Queen within me. The goddess beaten down and trampled on. Her glow slowly dimming until you came along. Now I remember who I am.
   -G.TW

WORTH THE JOURNEY

My expressions become beautiful impressions
Like a rose water milk bath relieving all your stresses
Fall into me and catch all my blessings
These are not words these are pure visions
I pour love into you because there's no tension
The more I give the more I receive
You may not know this, but my submission is key
I come back to you like the love of a mother's teed
Filling your belly
Filling your mind
Taking my time
Enjoying every moment
As I moor through time
Ride with me in my Sun boat as we see every edge of
my mind
Come float like the milky way and forget there's even
time
Find pleasure in seeing my true colors
For my spectrum is courageous like the great mothers
See my face and look into my eyes
Come with me cause I'm worth the ride
-C.A.T.

MAYBE IT'S ME

Feeling ignored by the world
    Unseen, unloved and overlooked
    Unbothered but deeply disturbed
    Your actions don't equal your words
    Where is the love you claim to feel?
    You move on and leave me on read,
    Or maybe just unread with no response,
    As you prioritise incoming messages.
    You are the most inconsistent,
    Filling me up with warm words,
    Emptying me out with cold actions.
    Our connection was so swift
    A single glance and touch
    And the sparks soared
    Past the heavenly plane
    To a universe beyond our imagination
    But it was just my imagination
    Cos you didn't look at me the same way
    Actually you just saw right past me
    Past my metaphorical existence
    To the corporal being beyond me
    And I'm left feeling ignored by the world
    Unseen, unloved and overlooked

Unbothered but deeply disturbed
-G.TW

BOREALIS

A King builds his universe then protects her gifts. An empty throne awaits with your name written in Sanskrit.

Yes beloved. You remember now don't you? You are very ancient, and very noble. You hold the greatest memories inside your opal. But first you must remember what it is to have a heart. You forgot how to love. You forgot what was taught.

Now you are back to make things right. To purify the worrisome faces that look like you in the night. You smile, you give, and your love's so bright. No corners, just beautiful round balls of glowing light. Surrounding my mind. Surrounding my life. My imagination is my guide as I walk in the moon light. Sunny stars and crazy eclipses. Solar flares and milky kisses.

I see nothing but heaven approaching in the distance.

-C.A.T.

Things that can't change:
My race
My age
My sexuality
My culture
My family

Things that can change:
Your mindset
-G.TW

ONCE UPON A TIME...

My heart shines through the winter like the last days of December. Flipping everything on it's head until we get a clearer picture. This life is not what you think sometimes it gets bitter. Are you going to be the light or just a fractal splinter? We are melanated beings vibrating from a center.

We spiral. We become. We implode. We are the stars riding in our great mother's abode.

Smooth sailing the magnetic waves of earth. Finding my way West where the Sun coronates my rebirth. I sail with ancient ones who know where to find our shore.

The absolute. The pure. The point. The zero.

I slayed the villain, road west, and became the hero.

-C.A.T.

MOTHER EARTH

O, winter sun
    You're my warmest friend
    Guarding my sanity
    Returning my joy
    And warmth to my core.
    I long to dance on the beach
    Feel the ground beneath my feet
    Connecting to mother earth.
    Come alive on the blanket
    Bringing an air of friendship
    Released from a basket of goodies.
    I'm in want of lighter layers
    Shedding the heaviness in my heart
    Building the heat just a fingertip away
    While I still long for the rain
    To take away this pain.
    -G.TW

UNIVERSAL SOULJA

Ancient ones make true intentions your reality
A wild dream once deferred is no longer their reality
They see how great we are becoming and they enjoy
our new reality
Letting go of old ways and all the major calamities
We are original so watching love grow is the
tendency
We do not fear healing ourselves or our frequencies
For we are no longer archon feed
But souldiers that protect the love mother earth
conceives
-C.A.T.

SLEEP PARALYSIS

You haunt my waking mind
    Such as you did my dreams
    Dreams so vivid and real.
    Scaring me so much during the day
    Infiltrating my peace at night
    My body could not reach the veil
    Searching for truth
    Paralysed in fear
    Feeling it so real
    This figment of my vivid imagination
    My heart beating in my throat
    I'm panicking, shaking, suffocating
    As you etch closer and closer
    My eyes fly open
    Still paralysed
    Trembling in fear
    Unable to scream or budge
    Fighting an internal battle
    Chasing freedom
    Emotions running chaotically away
    As you inappropriately use words
    And intimate actions
    Tied to my femininity
    Which I'm unable to explain

Or escape.
I fear my solitude
Like I fear being alone with you
But mostly I fear leaving her alone with you
Hoping you don't separate her familial ties
As you did with me and she who was older
Taking it too far with her
And just a little less with me
Crossing every line of comfort
Excused by your sick mind
Because I am her
Her is me and so is she
Invisibly restrained
Shackled so deep
A prisoner within myself
-G.TW

Go back
Way back in time
When gods roamed the earth
And you were an ancient being of the Divine
Look at your soul when you close your eyes
There is nothing but God inside
-C.A.T.

I don't wanna be loved like this,
    It's suffocating and painful.
    Cause I feel like I'm drowning in this,
    Mouth wrapped and pushed under water,
    Struggling to break free from this.
    Sharp pains attacking my poor heart.
    I don't wanna live like this,
    Insecure, paranoid and jealous.
    So I refuse to be loved like this,
    Slowly losing my breath over you.
    -G.TW

ISLAND OF FIRE

The ninja and the magician
The nightcrawler and the lotus blossom
The vertical vortex and the divine feminine
Together we sing a harmony sweeter than a million
beaches
Crashing on billions of crystals of sand
This is our magnificent plan
Feed the people with pure imagination until they
understand
Love is the only way to make your heart than a
feather again
-C.A.T.

SAVE ME

WAKING UP SHAKING,
My anxiety taking over my whole body,
And I can't breathe.
I'm suffocating and I can't see the light,
Can't feel the joy,
I'm struggling.
Sinking so deep into this mud hole,
My chest tight,
All hope is gone.
Tears streaming down my face,
Into my mouth choking me,
I can't breathe.
I can't sleep.
I can't think.
I'm trembling.
I CAN'T BREATHE!
Darkness consumes me.
Save me.
Save me.
Save me.
Can anyone hear me?
-G.TW

MY OAKLAND LOVE

MY LIFE IS an elegant story,
A trilogy that's etched in glory,
I find these moments to have less worry,
Harnessing the will to create a brand new story.
I hear the beautiful silence singing to me,
It feels like my mother's calling me,
My heart chakra ignites to melt the cold freeze,
I become still and begin to brew kundalini.
With this fire I manifest the will to bend all things,
With every element and every heartstring,
Watch how they answer to your voice,
Watch how their hearts sing.
Become the resting place for those who want to be
free,
Come lay on the strong arms of my mighty oak tree.
Paint your pain with my leaves,
Watch your guilt melt away with ease.
If you're lonely hold me close.
Take off your shoes and sit with me in the grassy
moss,
Close your eyes and get ready for love's liftoff.
-C.A.T.

2020 is the year I scroll through my phone
And the tears keep falling as I moan
A deep guttural groan
In vain
While in pain
-G.TW

MILLIONS OF MILES

I free my heart and I free my spirit,
　　I acknowledge my greatness in order to be it,
　　This is my birthright and the world's obsessed
with it.
　　My soul soars as a hawk to deliver this lovely
message,
　　Fear no one because humans have no leverage.

The key to my mind is a ring of emerald and gold,
　　I flow through time like the ankh I have been
shaped to mold,
　　Transcending to the ethers all around and making
my colors bold,
　　An original being that is no longer trapped by
humanities hold.

I let the caged bird free,
　　As my wings gleam with melanin beams,
　　Wielding the elements of this earth's
dimensionality.
　　A blur to most but unequivocally beautiful to
myself,
　　I create because I feel the need to spread
consistent wealth.

Come with me and create more joy with your
radiant smile,
The time is now for the children of the sun to
stretch for miles and miles…
-C.A.T.

BLOODLINE

SOME OF OUR ancestors got left behind on the
continent
    Only to experience pain like Genocide; King
Leopold and Apartheid
    Some of our ancestors jumped off the boats
    Because they preferred to die
    Than go forth with the life that awaited them
    Some of our ancestors were on boats that lead
them to new territories
    Only to experience Jim Crow right after Slavery
    All of our ancestors stood up for equality
    All of our ancestors hoped for a better future
    A freedom equal to those around us

Whether your ancestor stayed behind and avoided the
boats;
    Jumped ship or arrived fulfilling other's hopes
    All over the world negros are still suffering
    All over the world negros are still dying
    All this because of the shade of our skin
    We are all on the same boat and still fighting
    The oppression that was built as they were
colonising

May this fight today end with some systematic change
    Before our great grandkids suffer through the same things we're fighting for
    Since we're suffering through the things our great grandparents died for
    So how many times will history repeat itself before its deemed insane
    The cycle has got to end
    Black Lives Matter to no end
    -G.TW

How do I know vices are vicious?
We all know we have them,
Yet claim to admit this.
-C.A.T.

We don't care anymore
Whether people see how beautiful we are
'Cos that will always shine through
Cuts through all the violence and abuse
Because that ish is in our soul
And it's not going anywhere.
-G.TW

No bullshit,
Just show me love,
Give me a good story,
Or a real hug.
Simple things that make the heart sing like a dove.
-C.A.T.

KAFFIR

Why do I exist, Mama?
For the Whiteman says we are useless
Should I still raise my hand at school, Mama?
Even though the other kids call me stupid
When I try to help someone, Mama
They say I'm evil and corrupt
They say look at your skin
It's too dirty, go scrub yourself properly
They say I must go back to the bushes where I belong
They laugh at me, Mama, my big nose and bushy hair
They called me that bad word again
The one you said I must ignore
But I can still hear them in my head
Kaffir, kaffir, kaffir
I don't want to be black no more
I want to be the colour the world loves and
understands
I want friends who are friends with me for me
And not because we are the same race
I want to live, Mama
I want to live
-G.TW

A LIVING TESTIMONY

I used to think this world was full of trauma,
Until I discovered it was to make me love my
mamma.
I withstood the fire in order to cleanse all my drama.
I let my tears run down her back,
As her long braids become the gentle streams that
brought me back.
The rivers flow and I become the Bridge I was built
to be.
Connecting love in all directions so that we can all be
free.
This is a living testimony.
-C.A.T.

Everywhere in the world black people suffer; fight
and die
Just for the right to stay alive and have equality
-G.TW

THIS BLACK IS...

THIS BLACK IS beautiful, chaotic, yet personal.
    I search for little clues that might help me discover who I am,
    Because I've been blown across America like a desert sand,
    A storm I'm in the eye of currently,
    Every moment I think how I can acknowledge the pain and move flowingly?
    Through life so my little ones will know for certainty,
    Ol' Manhattan was given a life but said there's no folding in me,
    I picked up my cards and flipped them over,
    Only to show a bust in blackjack is a life that is seldom won over,
    Especially with this skin.
    Bleach it all I want,
    My soul wants what it wants,
    A true heritage to follow and live by,
    So that one day only joyful tears will cry,
    But that's inevitable,
    Because hardship is a part of this life,
    I've come to grips with it and made it my long lost wife,

Hopelessly romantic enough to never claim she's just a hot knife,

Slicing every which way to kill my might,
But this black skin will never be peeled,
Because it's in my soul that I feel,
It's in my hands when I snap,
It's in my smile when I laugh,
It's in my knees when I dance,
It's in my shoulders when I cradle,
It's in my mind when I create,
It's in my voice when I speak,
Just to say,
This black is beautiful, chaotic, and personal.

I see it as being gifted, cause it's the only way I can lift it.

-C.A.T.

Free your spirit from the limitations put on your soul
-G.TW

THAT BLACKNESS

WHY DOES IT feel like everywhere in the world
Black people are the most hated and tortured of
the world?
As colour deepens with every shade
The darkest of us made to live in shame
For what exactly?
To satisfy your need for control?
Who gave you dominion over our soul?
Or do you just not feel whole?
Our skin tone generating so much shade
Because our beauty within makes you afraid
We will not be made to feel ashamed
Or have our own power reclaimed
Apartheid you brought into our own land
Slavery when you took us forcefully to your land
King Leopold taking over Congolese lands
Injustice against Aboriginals in Australian lands
While lighter skin prevails in Asian lands
We're fighting to be black in our own countries
And fighting to be black in the land you took us to
But our culture, skills and art rejoiced
Until we fight to use our own voice
We will continue to set ourselves free
And if you're all for letting us be
Then you've nothing to fear

Cos we love whole heartedly
-G.TW

WATER BEARER

I am your reflection on distance shores,
    I am your lifeboat,
    I am your moor,
    I am your light source,
    I am your core,
    I project these intentions into the ethers to become
millions more.
    I stand in my own spotlight because I set the
stage,
    I brought in the lights and I burned through some
sage,
    They classify me as evil but I know my ways,
    I look darkness in the mirror to control my rage.
    Because this is my come up,
    This is my aquarian age.
    -C.A.T.

Love is joy and joy is love
-G.TW

THIS LOVE

I am limitless, I am gold.

I float through the heavens like petals from a rose. Gliding, soaring, while all so potent. I'm with you right now as I grow omnipotent. Making myself so incredibly small to whisper things into your ear. For they might seem strange, but eventually the symbols start to appear.

They tell me to stand up straight, to claim your name, and to claim your universe. Hold the crown steady even if it tilts a bit at first. This is a long lost journey. An awakening. A genetic reboot. Become an artist again with your magic super suit.

Fixate your mind and lock into the heavens. Then mold a life of beauty with sexy structure and silky pleasures. A place where we recognize the weather, the changes, and the seasons.

Come eat at the table and see why we share love for all reasons.

-C.A.T.

LONDON BAE

AFTER THE RAIN
>Came you
>My little rainbow
>Clearly not so little
>Bringing joy all around
>Your energy infectious
>Your smile delicious
>I love our talks
>Music sharing
>Until 3am you had me
>And we could hold on
>No ending that video call
>Til sleep overwhelmed us
>Then I remind myself
>That you're only temporary
>But it's ok
>You bring a smile to my face
>You brought the sun back
>Into my life it burns so bright
>So I'll enjoy you right
>Even for just this moment
>-G.TW

CLARITY

When I apply my entire will,
  Gateways become visible,
  The research becomes therapeutic,
  Knowing love becomes my weapon of tutelage
  When I start to remember the past lives,
  Visions answering those deep feelings of who am
I,
  Well, well,
  I can see the King thrives.
  He made it back to the throne with the triple black
mother by his side.
  In a world of chaos and in a world of madness,
  I found peace in her arms as she held my sadness.
  She knew I had seen the great fall,
  How it felt to once be so tall.
  So she wiped my tears and said go back home my
dear,
  For we have work to do and now your purpose is
clear.
  -C.A.T.

There's a duality in all of us that's fighting to be normal.
But what is normal?
-G.TW

ALCHEMICAL TRANSMUTATION

I CAN SEE the damage that they did to you,
So I fill my chambers with sage and crack a
window for you,
Remember mamma told us to do better?
Cause one day she'll be gone and we'll really
have to do better.
I know the shit hurts and sounds a bit bitter,
But what do you expect from a black boy seen as
a natural sinner?
This American shit got me fucked up,
So I turn my music up.
Drown out them mundane folks,
Or maybe I do it to scare them folks,
Press them up against reality like they did my
folks,
Got me thinking God ain't real and I should be
scared of my own cloak,
Only to find out we really are the greatest kinfolk.
And that American bitch gave us diaspora,
So we turned the fuck up and gave her high blood
pressure and asthma.
Bitch you better stay in that hospital bed, cause
once we find you ya dead…
That IV in your arm be giving you that good shit,
Making you think white privilege is the new shit,

But bet I unplug you and you start to lose it,

Cause all your ideas come from me I guess that makes me a nuisance,

You complain about bullshit and look completely foolish,

I think you just shit on yourself you smell stoolish,

Look America she's the truest!

I'll talk that shit and back it up with black bullets.

These are my words for those who think we still ignorant, and somehow grow into stupid.

White and black aren't the same, you just greyed out the pages,

Then splattered us with blood and said we are contagious.

How sweet it is to never be loved by a country you built,

And never got the chance to call it home cause you saw black people getting kilt,

It's still amazing that you don't have any guilt,

Maybe you don't wanna see or maybe the pussy in you won't let you conceive,

But this is my world and all we do is fucking bleed!

-C.A.T.

Love on me so hard my soul soars
-G.TW

ROSIE

ONLY YOU CAN make something so beautiful,
    Take what you know and create your musical.
    Find your soulmate and let them be your
harmony,
    Listen to the sunlight as it sings with me.
    Purifying your essence in order to get you back on
track,
    I'm the warrior that carries no weapons or traps.
    I walk this land and face my ankh toward heaven,
    I do this with will and I do this with my eleven.
    I don't look down anymore I just look up,
    I give myself all the audacity to fill my cup.
    For the great old ones know,
    We walk their footsteps from thousands of
millennia ago.
    I feel color when my eye lids close,
    I found peace when I became still as a rose.
    -C.A.T.

THE MELANIN WITHIN

THE MELANIN IN my soul is spiritual
 It has withstood King Leopold and Apartheid
 The melanin in my body is beautiful
 Big nose, bushy hair, don't care
 The melanin in my skin is powerful
 Surviving attempted murder through lynching and
whitening
 The melanin in my heart is bountiful
 Police please don't shoot; KKK please don't burn

The melanin in me
 Is tired of being shot at and raped
 Is through with society's misconceptions
 Is sick of your God complex
 And will not stay down
 Or keep quiet

We will rise up until the earth stops spinning
 Rise up until our bones stop shaking
 Rise up to turn the world upside down
 Rise up with the power of God within us

The melanin within me is
 Spiritual
 Beautiful

Powerful
Bountiful
-G.TW

SAILING WEST

Over my broad shoulders,
   The epitome of light shines and folds over,
   Meet me at the cusp is what I told her.
   So I grabbed my rubies and made my heart chakra
sing,
   This is beautiful, this is clean,
   This is perfect, this is truly serene.
   The waves of my mind are like the sounds of the
beach,
   I hear flutes blowing beneath the currents and the
coral reefs.
   Resurrect yourself like the Great Dead King,
   Moor west and gracefully become everything.
   -C.A.T.

I found the heart my soul was meant to love.
-G.TW

MA'S HOUSE

My King,
    I love you because the stories are true,
    You will a life of beauty because love is truth.
    I love you because you have so much work to do.
    In order to free our mind, love has to be the only favorite.
    I love you because I see the hypocrisy that needs to be eradicated.
    I love you because I wanted to heal and you showed me the trauma,
    I love you because you showed me the way back home to mamma's.
    -C.A.T.

BLISSFUL MISERY

(DEDICATED TO MANU Z. Prado)

All you see is Black and White
    Husband or wife
    While I see a spectrum
    A spectrum of light
    A spectrum of colours
    A spectrum of love
    The many shades of grey
    Should make me so blue
    But it's my choice to see the world anew
    What you don't understand
    You refuse to empathise
    What I don't feel
    I'm still forced to compromise
    Yet I stand in the middle of this road
    With your back turned to me
    I come here every night in my dreams
    While you continually walk away
    I'm left drowning in misery
    Sinking so blissfully
    But you don't care to see or feel
    Or even acknowledge my choice
    Which isn't a choice at all.
    -GTW

300

WALK WITH YOUR head up young man
    Pointed high toward the sky young man
    There's no need to look down young man
    For it's simply the ground young man
    Just keep going young man
    You'll soon find the wisdom of truth written in the
sand
    The journey is great and waiting on you young
man
    The empty throne awaits for the Sun to rise again
    Find your light in the dark so it may shine again
    The truth is stranger than it seems
    So hold true to your dreams
    Healers and magic workers of prosperity
    Learners and those willing to erase all the
negativity
    For a new destiny is awaiting our victory.
    -C.A.T.

NOTEWORTHY

It's with such joy that I write you this note
    Not sure why but I'm full of butterflies
    One day… two days… No response
    My message part of a new renaissance
    My heart sinks to the ground
    Suddenly my butterflies disappoint me
    Not sure why you still affect me this way
    Ignoring me like I'm not worth your day
    Not an hour, a minute or even a second
    Spare me the reasons while I pick up my heart
    Beat slowing as I watch it bleed
    -G.TW

That's all I count is growth,
I can't count anything else.
-C.A.T.

CAN I BE HEARD?

CAN I BE heard?
    Can I be listened to and understood?
    Why do I constantly have to repeat myself?
    Or feel like I'm always being dismissed?
    My opinions matter
    Stop calling me by that name
    It's not the one I respond to
    Don't put your finger in my ear
    I don't like it
    Don't envision me working in a bank
    It's not me
    I know you want the best for me
    But your wants don't align with my energy
    And even though I say so
    The first time never seems like it's enough
    Do you even know who I am as a person?
    Do you see or feel my soul?
    My overly emotional and creative spirit
    My love for peace and beauty
    My hopeful romanticism
    The way I surrender to nature and spirituality
    Getting in touch with my inner queen
    Practising mindfulness
    As I meditate and do yoga in the morning
    Journaling my life away.

I want to be remembered
I want to leave a mark on your heart
For you to remember that I was here
Because I am here
All flesh and bones
Curves in all the right places
Africa rooted so deep inside me.
My non-verbals are just as important.
So see me, hear me
The first time
And take note.
-G.TW

VELVET VINYLS

Sometimes my words just don't stop. So I close my eyes, and my mind takes me to the highest mountain tops. A magnificent journey high above the treetops. On ocean floors where you feel the warmth of the bedrock. And deep inside my heart where I see my beautiful mind and it's thoughts. Something like a movie you know? But this time I woke up and remembered I am not the villain, but the hero. And when I open my eyes, I seem to come back down to zero. Where love is at a point and so peaceful. Up and away is the only way to find peace. I saw you and thought wow what a magnificent peace. To see something grow is like watching a beautiful thing. I could write you a million poems off the life you breathe. A great mother standing before me, with a builder of worlds at your chest. We are the universe. We are the main track.

-C.A.T.

FUTURE ME, PAST YOU

SOMEDAY A MAN will come along
    He will love me for a minute
    Maybe a moment longer
    Or even a lifetime
    But he will treat me with care
    Remind me of what I deserve
    Cherish my entire being
    Kiss me like I'm his precious commodity
    Love me to heavenly bliss
    I'll understand all the poems
    All the love songs and movies
    I'll look back at what I had
    And know why I went though all that
    Because it led me to him
    He'll see the very core of me
    And remind me of my light
    While nurturing my worth
    He'll take me farther in a week
    Than the love I felt from you in a year
    But you showed it in your own way
    His will just collide with me with greater force
    Twin souls finally reuniting
    You were never wrong
    You were just wrong for me
    But I don't regret you

Because without you
I wouldn't be ready to welcome him
-G.TW

TWO TAILS

I AM THE big black cat lying in the tree,
   A tail that swings low in the jungle humidity,
   I dream observing nature and the worlds to be,
   I blend in with the shade but shine like the moon
with my beautiful eye,
   I see all things and decipher dimensions of the
blue sky.
   My tribe is tall,
   My tribe is quantum.
   I am the tallest peaks,
   I am the lava beneath your feet.
   I come from all things because the great mother
made me to be.
   She sits in a cave,
   Singing songs that warm the core of the earth,
   Waiting for the King to uncover his own
mysterious worth.
   He knows not what he is,
   He has been asleep while his kingdom has lost its
way.
   His crown sits right beside him as he
contemplates with wisdom,
   He looks for answers in silence in order to
visualize the prism.
   He is crystal and he is perfect,

He shines like the reflection of the sun on the earth's surface.

He is potent. He is dangerous.

He knows what love is and makes it contagious. Sometimes viral.

He steps out into the world and achieves more than mere survival.

He is a builder.

A bridge that cements many to their original title.

Holding keys to the force.

Shine young God,

Shine like you believe anything can be yours.

Become the affirmation you seek and the one who lights up any dark room.

For I am the red sun, and you are the blue moon.

-C.A.T.

NERVOUS

You once told me I make you nervous
    It's crazy how you articulated it
    Exactly the way I felt it
    The buzzing through my body
    The way you're so confident
    I thought it was only me
    I felt stupid for feeling nervous
    But you feel the same way
    And now I can't stop smiling
    My nervous makes you nervous
    G.TW

I loved you on purpose.
                    -G.TW

TWIN FLAME

Walk with me. For it's okay, and it's alright. Take your breaths, and take your time. I can feel the pressure mounted on your back and all down your spine. Stand up and let it fall like the crashing of a high tide. For years fear had a weight that kept you down and on a decline. But as the rains clear and the clouds part, I take heed and let this opportunity become mine. Grabbing life by the horns, I see the horizon of the sun at the perfect time. I am now sunshine. I am now in my mother's milky way. Following her lead to shores where rest awaits my name. Living forever in dimensions that bring love back to fame.

   -C.A.T.

2020 WAS

2020 WAS..
    Hopeful at first
    Heartbreaking at it's worst
    Started with year of the woman
    That leap year that will go down in history
    How we got here is a complete mystery
    COVID19 slipped into our vicinity
    Got us quarantined and in our vanity
    Killer Hornets popped up in the US
    Another thing we now had to finesse
    Are we in the book of Revelations?
    The world turning against us while we're facing
mass incarcerations
    Running for our lives being chased like Ahmaud
    Or maybe we should find safety in our homes
    But while we're peacefully asleep in our
sanctuary
    The police invaded and shot Breonna mercilessly
    Corona got me feeling like the outside air is
poisonous
    But the police out there also acting all ravenous
    My emotions overload and I feel suffocated
    I can't breathe I say suited up in my melanin
    I can't breathe he said laying on that tar floor

I can't breathe we screamed fighting for George
Floyd
I can't breathe we remember Eric Garner
Black Lives Matter we chant begging to end this
race war
Rainbow bodies protesting peacefully on this
universal floor
History repeating like the year of the Rodney
King fall
Curfews set in attempt to silence us all
But the rest of the world got our backs and picked
up the torch
They're marching out there while we reconvene
indoors
Together we'll march in solidarity as we've done
before
Systematic racism cycle no more
Hands Up. Don't Shoot.
And it's only June
-G.TW

KNIGHTS OF THE ROUND TABLE

I have committed no crimes. Matter of fact, it isn't even mine. But I'm the one who brings it life. It's my spirit you see. I flipped everything on it's head, now there's no good or bad, or right or wrong. My purpose is to understand love as the greatest weapon of all. In 30 years I've witnessed it all. Every type of pain and every type of fall. So when I make my universe, there will be no shame. There will only be water flowing in between the trees, and shooting high above the heavens. That's where you'll find me and all my elevens.

    -C.A.T.

Sometimes I feel like I give and give,
And when I'm in need,
Those same people laugh in my face.
No wonder Riri said "Once a good girl goes bad,
she's gone forever,"
Because that might soon be the case.
-G.TW

GOLDEN TIME OF DAY

This universe is secretly ours,
    As soon as you let go,
    You hear the voices of all the flowers,
    Singing a love song that takes you much higher,
    The sweet sound of silence and it's beautiful
desires,
    It wants peace and it wants this message to be
kindled in the fire,
    That love is real and that's the only true empire,
    And if you cherish love's deeds,
    You can travel anywhere your heart leads.
    Yes indeed,
    I patiently wait for the magnificent day,
    To give those who stand next to me,
    These golden sun rays.
    -C.A.T.

4202020

THROUGH MY HIGH is my reflection
While I connect to my intention
Releasing your hold is my affliction
Trying but I'm stuck in this position

How do you still make me smile like that
Catch me reminiscing unlike a doormat
Maybe my battery's running flat
While you make my heart so fat

Beautiful disaster Collide
Bonafide/ Pride
Legacy
Jealousy/ Ecstasy

So fast you were on to the next one
As if you didn't care about me as your past one
I realise I may need therapy
For still thinking you are my remedy
-G.TW

The music...it sounds so beautiful.
                                    -C.A.T.

DAILY THOUGHTS OR THOUGHTS DAILY

Sometimes I look in the mirror and I don't recognise the face staring back at me. There's a smile on her face that my mouth can't reach, a light in her eyes but all I feel are tears bubbling under the surface, an excitement running through her body while I tremble in fear. When you're around her you feel the joy dripping from her pores while all I feel is pain and darkness.

I stare at myself acknowledging the failure that I am. Appreciative of the life I have been given but feeling like I'm standing in one spot wanting to move forward but unaware of how to. Standing on a ticking time bomb. Scared of how my family is fearing for my future. No direct line or path to the goals I want to achieve.

Am I talented enough?
>   Am I working hard enough?
>   Am I enough?

I remember that there's a whole world outside of me. So I plaster on her face as my mask and gather the strength to make it through this day.

   -G.TW

ADOLESCENCE

I AM WHOLE.

I bring my world together with feminine beauty
and masculine gold.

I am the shadow that wants to know what the
lights hold.

Are you a driving force that can't be denied,

Or a follower that doesn't know his kind?

Keep your spirit divine, and what you seek is
already inside your mind.

These are simply words from my creative intuition,

It once wasn't and now it's my clearest intention.

It takes a great soul to be a King.

He has to know wisdom like his wife,

And have courage the moment he steps in the
ring.

Gleaming and growing everything he touches,

When he needs peace he aligns himself within his
mother's clutches.

For she speaks highly of him and recommends his
presence,

He's the one who will protect love and it's
essence.

A toast to the King, for he has learned his lessons,

Earning his empty seat through the stages of adolescence.

-C.A.T.

I learnt to love myself fully
Even when I felt incomplete
-G.TW

AFFIRMATION #5

I stand out like the sun.

One day that is what you will become. Shining light and giving life to everything you see. Making yourself mighty by mastering lower frequencies.

This is why they call you Sun. You scorch bad habits and make them shine like candy paint when it's done. This is because we are one, but before one comes absolutely nothing. And when you're absolute, you will reach the shores that blow a thousand flutes. Willing yourself to glory has made everyone proud of you.

So celebrate today and for all eternity. Your mind has been cleansed. Your soul has been set free.

-C.A.T.

Always felt like the black sheep
My family's unapologetic creative
A free spirit reined in by structure
Fighting to fly
Needing to soar
-G.TW

GAME OF THE CENTURY

Don't be sad about where I'm going,
Take your worries and cast them into the
knowing,
For I am free and feel God flowing,
I come to recognize I am rowing.
Gently, gently, around this watery planet,
I've crashed every shore and beat every bad habit.
I'm dying to reach auroras lights that lead to
heaven,
Life flashing before my eyes because the feeling
is pleasant.
I find my way home at the point of pure silence,
Where thoughts are manifested and peace
conquers violence.
I pitched myself the greatest game but had a no
hitter in the process,
A mind of polarities and a life of progress.
-C.A.T.

THE JOYS OF LOVING A MAN

I DON'T WANT to feel this way anymore
   I'm so angry
   So angry
   And mad
   Frustrated
   Heartbroken
   Sad
   I want to scream
   WHY?!!!
   WHY ME?
   How were we so right
   Before things went so left
   What did I do wrong?
   But I didn't do anything wrong
   She just did everything right
   And I may always love you
   Cos I fuck with you as a person
   So there's mad love there
   But right now
   I'm pissed
   I'm siiiick
   So fucking mad
   That I can't have you
   I hate this so much
   So fucking much

I hate this
I hate you
I love you.
-G.TW

THE WESTERN INN

I FIND MY life quite beautiful,
    I sit and stare as I start to ooze with you. I feel myself melt and feel the earth do it too. It breaths and I breath too. We dance the breath of life and let ourselves roam nature's cues. We understand it's rhythm, we understand it's blues. We keep our minds still to create spectacular hues.

    Like wine, creating a natural chemical that brings you face to face with your melanin timeline. Are you alive or are you just waiting for stimulation for the hundredth time? Same story, same timeline.

    Is it groundhog day or do you see a change in who you are? Does the world frighten you or can you see it as your own? Do you feel everything you do is magnificent or just a heavy stone?

    Can you see the journey and make it appear as an oasis? Tucked away in the mirage of a thousand different places. But never once did it move it just stayed the course. The discipline, the data, the electro-magnetic force.

    The pyramids, the labyrinths, and the fiery iron core. My DNA throbs as I truly want to know more. My destiny is not money nor is it impressing you as I walk through doors. I'm just being god in human form. Correcting my lows and making them my new highs. Making a rightful order of things and doing it with my mind.

Born in the new age, but billions of years old. I came to resurrect the Dead King's throne.

-C.A.T.

If you're unable to turn the black and white in your life to colour then perhaps you are living in the wrong dimension and waiting for some sort of ascension? There's polarity in all of us, one minute we are creating the universe while in the next we are out here destroying it. How do you vibrate amongst that transitional colour weathering through the seasonal storm to get to that season of bliss?
  -G.TW

GOOD MORNING SUNRISE

AS I SIT and watch the unusual,
　　I see that my life is finally beautiful.
　　My eyes roll back and I flip this world upside
down,
　　I see it's true nature and therefore I am heaven
bound.
　　Hear as my voice shakes through the ethers,
　　I am the one who brings the message,
　　Therefore I am the keeper.
　　A son of the great Sun,
　　A star from the highest realms of heaven.
　　A seed that cannot be destroyed,
　　A threat since the age of seven.
　　I break through stereotypes and I break through
disease,
　　I bring my people to shore with hearts that glisten
green.
　　Hand me my crown I have seen it through my
eye,
　　I have given my house a name that will light up
the skies.
　　No more dark days,
　　No more worries,
　　For I am the morning sunrise on that boat to
glory.

-C.A.T.

WHAT IS MY LEGACY?

What is my legacy?
    I want to carve a path full of transparency
    Bringing others joy and pure ecstasy
    Rising to every occasion with no jealousy
    Putting ingredients in to create my own recipe
    But even then there is no guarantee
    So first I gotta check my mentality
    Hold my own hand to gain my own prosperity
    While God has paved the way for my destiny
    As I fight the hurdle that is white supremacy
    But I will get through it even if it's independently
    My ancestors out there looking all heavenly
    After fighting through the same battle must be
heresy
    So my friends go around looking for that
Hennessy
    Because as black people there is no other therapy
    It's either that or them driving us to commit a
felony
    While the fairer keep pitting us as their enemy
    So I hope this poem provides them clarity
    Where we can all come together to find the
remedy
    Since as humanity there is unity in poetry

And that so happens to be my specialty
So I have to view myself as a rarity
And that's the start of my legacy
-G.TW

THE BUILDER

I've gone through every emotion,
   And it's finally time to rise.
   I'm leaving everything on this earth behind,
   Except love.
   My soul will rejoice,
   I am my mother's finest choice.
   Dipped in gold,
   And then cloaked in melanin.
   Charged with fire,
   And hardened to a point past earthly desires.
   Because I build stars.
   Because I build empires.
   -C.A.T.

I feel like I'm nobody's priority.

Maybe it's time I submit to myself.
-G.TW

THIS IS IT

LIKE THE RIVERS that flow downstream,
You will soon hear how the ocean rings.
A soft harmony that every body needs,
Dark moon waters that whisper my creed.
Moored to the place of peace where my ancestors
wait by the shore,
Where everything comes to a point and I implode
from the core.
I am Quantum. I am 4.
The mothership watches and sees you are worthy,
I tend the herd to become the star I want to be.
No one soothes water the same way,
They crash, they splash, they flow with haste.
Yet sometimes they come to an opening,
And float lazily in the middle of the lake.
So when the journey comes I will gladly make my
way,
For I have learned there is only one way.
I see stars and I see DNA,
Etched in past lifetimes from which I did
meditate.
Find the light and you will find your gift,
The throne is empty and awaits for you to grow
spiritually rich.
Because no matter what you think,

This is it.
-C.A.T.

SUBMISSION

Do you know what it means to really submit to love
    To open your heart and let someone in
    Intentionally and gently
    Caring about their entire being
    Feeling protective over them
    Planting kisses all over their body
    Loving them unconditionally
    Breathing in their essence
    Taking time to check in
    Is this ok
    Are you ok
    Tell me what you like
    Tell me what you don't like
    This is a safe space for you to be honest
    Pure love seeping through your pores
    Really seeing them
    While they completely see you
    Freedom to live
    Freedom to love
    Heart's on fire because we are the flame
    Mind, body, soul
    Love so gentle you can't let go
    An all consuming submission
    -G.TW

TRANSCENDENTAL MEDITATION

Granted when it gets bitter,
My inner fire starts to churn and make wisdom
it's center.
Foresight blended perfectly with forethought,
What I thought was impossible has now grown
enough stalk.
The anchor of the relay meditating on the golden
baton,
In striking position ready to accelerate through the
aeons.
Crushing my enemies with anticipation and a
brilliant gold mind,
Tapped into a frequency of imagination and
irrelevance for time,
This is how I become less body, more mind,
I simply leave my addictions behind,
I cut off their heads like treacherous Kings of past
times,
For I am a King at the Royal Table,
We speak these words so that you no longer
believe in fables.
    -C.A.T.

I despise asking for help.
And sometimes when I do ask,
I remember why I hate it.
Such unkindness often shocks me.
-G.TW

POLAR EXPRESS

Same time cycle,
    Different mindset.
    The time used to tick,
    Now time bows to my discipline.
    My mind takes a long beautiful journey,
    And when I come back I am whole and much
more worthy.
    These are my stories,
    Wrapped tightly and spiraling within my core.
    I say these words through stomach aches and even
when my body's sore.
    That is when we become much more,
    Will oozing from every pore,
    75 trillion cells distinctively on board,
    Headed straight to the mothership where our kind
is adored.
    -C.A.T.

MY 6 IS YOUR 9

I THINK IT'S important to accept and respect
    That we can neither limit or expect
    Other's views of society
    Based on our own notoriety
    The background and experience that inform us
    Get swallowed by news and opinions not for us
    Even those closest to us
    May argue their defense against us
    Their personality and energy clashes against ours
    Sinking me into oblivion for hours
    Doubting my passions and my empathy
    Making it hard for me to find any serenity
    Even our own siblings judge our every step
    Brutally breaking me down even as I prep
    Making me wonder if I'll get past your
disapproval
    Are you brutally honest or just honestly brutal?
    My 6 is your 9 is what we agree to disagree
    But without you walking in my footsteps
    Your first instinct is still to be judgmental
    So I'll just accept we're on two different pages
    Secretly thinking you're stuck in the middle ages
    But my love for you goes beyond all phrases
    -G.TW

You want the perfection rather than the inspiration.
Your wires got crossed, now you need to master
meditation.
-C.A.T.

Walk with the mindset of a driver,
Drive with the mindset of a pedestrian.
-G.TW

ALWAYS REMEMBER

Iron ropes moor me to my destination,
I travel the smooth waters to await my
celebration,
For this is a coronation,
Every cell in my body knew I had the patience,
To join my ancestors and enjoy my universal
creation,
A world full of wonder a world full of nations.
All united and all singing the same song,
The song of our mothership hums and speeds
along,
We are fantastic, we are like no one else,
When you find this story in your mind,
Make sure you never put it back on the shelf.
Your life has been made so you can finally love
yourself.
I'll see you soon so be well,
For death and life are the same when you remove
the illusions of hell.
-C.A.T.

SOARING HEART

I've been thinking about being found
    How I'm lost in the wake of my dreams
    My body walking through this earth
    While my soul is in search of something
    Something greater, something profound
    I cannot pinpoint exactly what it is
    But I know it is restless of the daily complexities
    The inaction brought on by the victimless
    I'm floundering in a pool with edges and corners
    Suffocating my entire view of society
    Are we not women of honour?
    Are our hearts so unattainable?
    Something about the way we are held
    The way in which we move and dance
    The way my curves flow into how I'm rooted
    In the way the earth keeps me feeling tall
    My spirit freely flying high in the wind
    Escaping the flames taking over the planet
    Or how the earth shakes when I think of you
    I can't control my mind as it escapes this reality
    Living in the dream of you and I
    An escapade we feel but cannot touch
    You've pierced my very soul you see
    In ways even poetry can't decipher

I'm lost in your eyes and smile
That very dimple reserved for me
Your laugh, your accent, that intense gaze
The way you make my soul smile
Or how you hold back your words for me
Checking in on my comfortability
But with you I want to feel grounded
So won't you come and find my soaring heart.
-G.TW

FIRE & DESIRE

I'm made for the journey.

    This is the last leg. I felt it in my weak knees as a kid. I felt it in my gut that I was a God. I felt different. I felt chosen. I felt like a million eyes were on me. A tall King. A wise King. Don't slouch your posture. Embrace everything. Look at your surroundings. Feel the essence of the great mother coursing through you. Ready to burst this place into a billion pieces to recollect love and become it's perfection. I will never fall again, I will look under every rock, in every corner, in every hood, in every concrete jungle, my Oakland jungle. Come tussle. Come battle. I find my peace in facing the world with my eye open, and my heart pure as blue fire. Walk with me son, let me show you how to inspire.

    -C.A.T.

Yo did you hear about the capitol insurgency?

Yooooo 2021 is off to a crazy start. That shit was wild.

But was it though? What did we think all this shit was leading up to?

"Stand back and stand by," he said.

What did we think that shit implied?

Black people out here fighting for their lives but you threaten a democracy because you are feeling butt hurt over your candidate losing. Not coming to terms with it got your mind twisted and it's all confusing. The Natives said it best, this what they did to us so they're just turning on each other. So since this ain't your land, you struggle to keep your feet on the ground and lose the humanity that inspires us. May the rest of us lose sight of the teachings of our inferiority because we are seven days in and our refund and exchange date has expired. Man, maybe I should censor myself to impress, 'cos they've deported people for much less.

-G.TW

AFFIRMATION #44

As I near my cycle of life I am born again. Under no names, and under no clan or kin. For I am original, and finally without skin.

No longer trapped. No longer confused. I find my melody in the laughter that I choose. It is loud and it is free. It rings with an exclusive harmony. Only those who have the right frequency can hear me. No matter how far I project or how many times I beg you. If you don't see it for yourself, the universe will never let you.

You can't be King without the vision. If you intend to lead then you intend to make decisions. Ones that will alters lives for generations to come. So it is only right that I write this affirmation.

It gives me life, it gives me the truth.

I have all the pieces of a masterpiece built. I will make this castle in honor of those who once had this world built. Who shifted energy in the etheric fields. Use your mind to move what seems like impossible objects. Crush them like giant waves hitting Hawaii's doorstep.

Creating new life at the point of magma and water. Creation comes when you've learned how to love her. For I am beauty and I am wisdom. I manifested to create a million years of peace for my kingdom.

This is what I call true freedom.

-C.A.T.

LOVE, FIND ME IN THE MORNING

Love, find me in the morning
    When the day breaks
    Of warm red and royal orange
    Where the world is silent
    And nature breathes peacefully
    Where some dreams are alive
    While others silently ending
    When my mind is undisturbed
    By the cruelties of this world
    Where my heart meditates
    Connecting to all eight chakras
    When my whole being is present
    Living in the Now, all anxieties subsided
    Where sleeping babies begin to coo
    And mothers arise finally rested
    When the world is at pause
    Just for a second, just for a minute
    Where stillness reigns
    And chaos unimaginable
    When my fingertips brush yours
    Ever so slightly as my body awakens
    Where my soul has travelled
    A million miles to a million adventures

Where hope is singing softly
Songs of beauty and grace
Where inspiration lays beneath the surface
Biding its time
Waiting to be set free
Love, find me at my happiest
Find me drenched in sorrow
Just as long as you find me.
-G.TW

My life is a miracle.
-C.A.T.

I'm here waiting for you to let me in.
Signed, Your Joy.
-G.TW

I'LL BE

When you see my ashes you'll finally see,
    That I am no longer singular.
    Put your hands in the ashes,
    And grab a bit of my universe.
    Sprinkle me near my favorite places,
    And see how countless I become.
    I am everywhere,
    I sense those are happy tears,
    And some are because you are scared,
    But remember our love and you will never have to
fear.
    The time is now,
    And the future they talk about will never come
down.
    You are the only key,
    So when you feel lost,
    Close your eyes and feel my essence.
    Listen as my voice whispers your blessings.
    Know this the beginning of something great.
    I'll be right here to help,
    I'll be right here to keep you straight.
    -C.A.T.

TORNADO KISSES

Today was a hard day.
    For someone always seeing the best in people,
    I struggled with it a lot today.
    But it's ok.
    I let the tears flow,
    Submitting to my pain and anger.
    Frustration swirling inside me,
    Like a tornado.
    I let it gently blow kisses through me,
    But I won't let it swallow me whole.
    Inhale.
    Exhale.
    Breathe.
    Today was a hard day,
    But I'll be ok.
    -G.TW

I KNOW YOUR SECRET

I HAVEN'T BEEN real on how much I've missed you. You see I love you so
   much but it started to get really heavy....and I didn't know why. You just couldn't answer my questions when we talked and that made me wonder why. I figured it was done and I had solved you and this whole thing out. So I let love sink to the bottom and that's the one thing I needed to climb back out.

   You see I have a story greater than any man, or any mind can carry. It all started when she guided me to the river of the many. She holds my hand and tells me to see it a different way where there's plenty. Where things come full circle and no one knows it, but you're winning. And maybe you didn't realize it but your daddy was missing.

   All the time. He made me search for my own love inside and now I no longer vent. I just crush myself into a fine powdered incent. Then I burn slow to finally understand the whole shit. To finally know your secret.

   You had no friends, you had no keepers. You tried to find love, but your shadows became the deceivers. You should have ran with love instead of trashing it. You would have found peace on the other side of it. If only you would take care of it. I know your secret and I'm no longer scared of it.

    -C.A.T.

I think most people don't realise how sensitive I
actually am.
I guess my poker face deceives me sometimes
too.
-G.TW

PRETTY THOUGHTS

I WRITE BEAUTIFUL words of art,
   Twisting and turning and becoming what I
thought.
   The page is never blank because words come
down heaven's staircase.
   I hear whispers of this and that,
   So I grab my pen and pad.
   I can't let my intuition just fly by,
   So I stop all things on a dime.
   I live in the zone but I'm never conflicted.
   I close the door behind me and ride the wave of
eternal liquid.
   I cross the ocean and see a shore full of
prosperity,
   Walking into a new world where my memory
banks are full of clarity.
   It can seem farfetched if you haven't got a map,
   Especially if you haven't laid your head back.
   I see stars when I close my eyelids,
   You can see now why God resides inside
my pyramid.
   For I am, and that makes us two,
   We harmonize to reveal the full spectrum of our
hue,

Making royalty from the electricity of our melanin hue.

The body is pure and hereto comes my mind,
I became a scientist through electric alkaline.
I'm so elastic I could slip through time,
A smooth transition through black holes like my great mother Divine.

She sits and waits for me to endure my time,
For when I am ready,
She will hand me the keys,
And float us across the sky.
-C.A.T.

Let me plant kisses on your soul
Seeding your soil
Nurturing your heart.
-G.TW

ROMANTIC SKY

FIND YOUR FOOTING on this steep mountain,
Facing rocky cliffs and swirling winds.
Finding my footing like a goat in his sure-footed stance.
I don't guess or take the chance.
I see my percentages, adjust my geometry, and just execute my plan.
To become one then become millions.
Filling hearts with love that pours down in between clouds.
Opening third eyes and purifying souls.
My heart sings a song made of gold.
Vibrating through everything and breaking it down to a single point,
Becoming everything I is how I fell in love with Sun,
Will I fall in love with myself of just say I'm done.
Do I relax or do I strain into the climb,
It's my decision so honestly it takes time.
But my time,
And this time,
There won't be a next time,
Just fine wine and dinner time.

And sunrises that show rainbows and coloured skies.
A romantic sky.
-C.A.T.

KING TO MY QUEEN

SHALL YOU SAVE me thus?
    Whispering yes through music
    As my spirit arises
    Planting itself in your soil
    Shall you renew me thus?
    Have you a claim on my soul?
    As a lover through the ages
    Have you no pity
    Invading my sanctuary
    Arising the bloom in my soul
    Consuming every fibre of my being
    How shall I love thee?
    My darling flame
    Igniting butterflies
    Discovering a wealth of purity
    Like a dark mist you transcend
    Devouring me with your words
    Fare thee well on your journey to me
    I await for your arrival in my royal court
    Where you shall bare the burden of my affection
    Whet my appetite with your words
    As is your duty to win me with poems
    Shall you be the conqueror of my heart?
    And thus quench my scorching fire
    Or shall you be a serpent so venomous

As to poison the life in my veins?
-G.TW

Be who you are and don't change.
Only then will you find what you're looking for.
What your soul has been looking for.
And that is simply to find your way back home.
-C.A.T.

NO RHYME THIS TIME

I THINK I lost myself.
    I'm not exactly sure when or how,
    But one moment I knew exactly who I was.
    The next moment I'm looking in the mirror,
    Staring at a stranger.
    I recognise the features on my face,
    But I can't find the soul beneath my eyes,
    Or the pep in my step.
    I don't sing in the shower anymore.
    I don't even know where the time goes,
    While I stand there letting the water run.
    There's an emptiness I can't describe,
    And I was so sure of myself.
    Sure of the person I was,
    Sure of the path I was taking.
    I put in the work,
    I had the vision,
    But life wouldn't work with me.
    I knew my calling.
    I knew what I was supposed to do,
    Where I was supposed to go.
    But one day I questioned myself,
    I listened to what others said,
    And I got lost in their ideas of me.
    Perceptions of a comfortably conservative life,

But that was never me nor for me.
My spirit flies in the night time,
Landing in colours and beauty,
Beyond our imagination.
I was never meant to be tied down.
The earth was mainly a power source,
Recharging my flame,
Before I traveled to a new land.
And this was my path.
A never-ending journey.
But as I'm being pulling to the ground,
I feel dead inside,
Caged in in a foreign land.
A spectacle to admire,
For your temporary high.
-G.TW

QUADRILLION

It never stops, so we never stop. We burst through black holes to get back to the top. When my body is no longer needed, my soul carries me safely to the shores of my own eden. Where family awaits my grand rising. As I walk out of the rushing river and lay on the banks of my own history, I peacefully see the sun with my own eye. To enjoy nothing but the pure love I have found inside. This is how we thrive. We strip ourselves of our worries and elevate on high. There is no institution that could tell you why. You have to just know deep down inside. That we are more, we are millions. We are quantum, we are quadrillion.

    -C.A.T.

My mind is in the future but my heart is in the past.
-G.TW

SOULMATES

Do you see my color?
Do you see my muse?
Do you hear the melody that plays my tune?
And when the silence begins to subdue,
Hold my hand through the drought,
So when it rains we don't drift about.
I'll swim through tidal waves to bring your love
safely ashore,
Restoring life into your breast and singing you the
sweetest chord,
How heavenly it is to find the true source.
I see your color,
I see your muse,
I am the one who falls in love with you.
-C.A.T.

HOME

I feel the most at home
　　Laying in your arms
　　Grazing the softness of your lips
　　Caressing the warmth of your skin
　　Surrounded by the sweet scent
　　Love swimming in the air
　　Soaking up all my troubles
　　Your smile is my happiest place
　　Your eyes speak a language I cannot resist
　　Your words cut me deeper that anyone else
　　But your heart loves harder
　　I'm drowning in you
　　Floating in you
　　Breathing in you
　　Peace and serenity
　　Fire and passion
　　Love
　　Home.
　　-G.TW

LET IT SHINE

Discipline is my sweet chariot.
    It carries me through deep revelations.
    I find myself constantly bucking the system,
    Yet this time I'm doing it with grace and wisdom.
    The worries are slowly starting to melt away,
    As I burn through them like calories on a hot day.
    My mind has solidified it's direction,
    No judgment, jealousy, or consuming discretion.
    I found all this peace through stillness and
reflection.
    So I love my reflection.
    I start to smile at the smallest affections.
    It builds my confidence and allows more in this
direction.
    I start to recognize those Kings trained to protect
their women.
    Making their sweet chariots out of pure discipline.
    To all gods who currently walk as men,
    I salute you and hope your joy shines from within.
    -C.A.T.

Thank you for being the reason
I wake up with a smile on my face.
-G.TW

The Great Mother Lives.
-C.A.T.

FREE ME

FREE ME FROM my shackled dreams.
Free me from their adjuring eyes.
Free me from their minuscule thoughts,
Caging in my soul,
As my spirit flies higher than their vision.
Free me from injustice and inequality.
Free me from your perception of life.
We are not one vision nor mindset.
My restrictions don't apply to you,
So keep yours to yourself.
My body my struggles my pain my choice.
Free me from my insecurities,
Keeping me grounded in anxiety,
While I was born to soar.
Free me from extremists,
Whipping me from all sides,
As I carry the scars on my back.
Free me from this prison,
Where who one chooses to lay with,
Is a topic of controversial discussion.
Free me from small minds.
Free me from small lives.
Free me from you.
Free me from me.
Free me.

-G.TW

THE BUTTERFLY EFFECT

I am peace.
I walk this earth gently and intentionally.
Gliding through the air like a butterfly that has just
hatched free.
I am clean and I am brilliant.
I shine as every ray of sunshine energizes my wings.
With every flutter I create great things.
-C.A.T.

I miss the spring in my step,
You gave me during the summer.
But not how hard the fall was,
When you left me in the winter.

-G.TW

HOE IS LIFE

See what you did, kid?
    Run me dirty
    Disrespecting me
    Now they gon' miss out
    Of what you dished out
    None of this good good
    'Cos now hoe is life
    Taking a hold of my sexuality.
    You broke my heart
    So Imma hold onto the pieces
    Watch me fulfil my needs
    Physical satisfaction
    Emotional distraction
    I feel sorry for the next guy
    Who aims for my heart
    'Cos no matter what he'll miss
    Miss me with all that shit
    He is not my ex
    And that I'll accept
    He may be different from the rest
    But he still won't survive
    This wasn't me
    Was never my vibe
    But Jazzy and Gabi said it well

"You're gonna make a hoe outta me"
-G.TW

A COMPLETE REVELATION

It's the heart's journey.

Will you find peace and let yourself implode?

Or will you let the terrors of the day identify your core and cause you to explode?

The choice is simple. There are only two.

But can you get over the mental hurdles too?

Stop shape-shifting and stand still for a moment.

If you feel the silence then maybe you'll start to own it.

For there is nothing out there greater than you,

Only your perspective can change that view.

You have to gaze into your reflection and see what really matters,

And that only comes when your peace no longer scatters.

You become more than just an explanation,

You start to remember what you used to be.

A complete creation.

A quantum revelation.

-C.A.T.

I CAN'T BREATHE

I CAN'T BREATHE
    He said
    With a knee pressing on his neck
    I can't breathe
    She thought
    As the bullets hit her sleeping body
    I can't breathe
    He said
    Being chased around on his morning run
    I can't breathe
    I thought
    My chest exploding from all this violence
    I can't breathe
    I said
    Hurting for all my brothers and sisters
    I can't breathe
    I thought
    Terrified for this life growing inside me
    I can't breathe
    We cried
    Burying the innocent lives we've lost
    I can't breathe
    We chanted
    Rising up for all our black lives
    I can't breathe

He said
I can't breathe
She said
I can't breathe
We said
I can't breathe
It hurts
-G.TW

R.I.P.

I can't breathe.

Stop Asian Hate.

Say her name.

R.I.P TO GENDER VIOLENCE VICTIMS IN
SOUTH AFRICA:

ABENISE BOWES / AGNES MZISA / AGNES
NDLOVU (DLAMINI) / ALEXA VILJOEN /
ALEXIA NYAMADZAWO / ALICE LOTTER /
ALICIA NYAMANZAWO / ALIME MBASHA /
ALLISHANDRE "SHANDRE" FLOORS / ALICE
MAREE / ALLISON PLAATJIES / ALTHEA
SPIRES / ALTHENA MALGAS / ALTECIA
KORTJIE / RAYNECIA KORTJIE / ALYSSA
BOTHA / AMAHLE QUKU / AMANDA MILA /
AMANDA MNGONYAMA / AMANDA
MTHEMBU / AMELIA JANSEN / AMILA KAWA /
AMBER STRYDOM / AMINA ABRAHAMS /
AMY BIEL / ANDISWA ZWENI / ANDREA
VENTER / ANEEQAH FAKIER / ANELISA

DULAZE / ANENE BOOYSEN / ANGELA
MARINUS / ANGELIQUE CLARK-ABRAHAMS /
ANGELIQUE HARMSE / ANGELIQUE VANESSA
PATTENDEN / ANIKA SMIT / ANNISI MEYE /
ANISHA VAN NIEKERK / ANNA FRANCINA
KRUGER / ANNA VD MERWE / ANNATJIE DU
PREEZ / ANNATJIE MYBURGH / ANNCHEN
FERREIRA / ANNE MARIE AYLWARD / ANNE
FOUCHE / ANNE ROEBERT / ANNERIE
GROBLER / ANNETTE KENNEALY / ANNI
DEWANI / ANN-MARI WAPENAAR / ANSIE
STEYN / ANTHEA THOPPS / ANTOINETTE
BOTHA / ANZUNETTE DU PLESSIS / ARIN
ESTERHUIZEN / ARINA MULLER / ARVITHA
DOODNATH / ASANDA SIYOKO / ASHIKA
SINGH / AVIWE JAMJAM / AVIWE WELLEM /
AYAKHA JIYANE / SPHESIHLE MPUNGOSE /
KHWEZI MPUNGOSE / KUHLEKONKE
MPUNGOSE / AYESHA KELLY / BABONGILE
NZAMA / BABY C / BABY DANIEL / BABY
JORDAN LEIGH NORTON / BABY LAGELIGHLE
/ BABAY LUMKA MAKASI / BANDILE
SKOSANA / BELINDA ERIKA WERNER / BELLE
EDWARDS / BERYL LAMBERTH / BERYL
MORGAN / BETH TOMLINSON / BIANCA GOSH
/ BIANCO LINO MCGOWAN / BIANCA
MATROOS / BIANCA PARSONS / BONGEKA
MGQOBOZI / BONGEKA PHUNGULA /
BONGEKILE NTENZA / BONGISWA
MAJIKIJELA / BOTSHELO MOTSOMI / BRENDA
FAIRHEAD / BRENDA JOHANNES / BRENDA
RWANDO / BUKEKA SIGUNGQA / BUSISIWE
BUSI NGWADLA / CAMERON BRITZ /

CANDICE BARTMAN / CARA AUSTEN
JENKINS / CARLY ISAACS / CARMELITTA
BAATJIES / CAROL FABRIEK / CAROL
PIENAAR / CAROLINE JACOBS / CAROLYN
FRARA / CATHERINE (CATHY) IRVING /
CATHERINE KROG / CATHY VAN
COPPENHAGEN / CATHY PURDON / CAYLINN
LINKS / CECILE POTGIETER / CECILE SMIT /
CELINE SMITH / CELINE COWLEY / CERI
DUVENHAGE MCCRAE / CHANEL DU TOIT /
CHANELLE HENNING / CHANTELLE BORCHER
(LEENDERTZ) / CHANTELLE MATTHYSEN /
CHANTAL DEAN / CHANTAL MAKWENA /
CHARMAINE CANNINGS / CHARMAINE
CONRADIE / CHARMAINE MARE /
CHARMAINE PIERS / CLAUDINE RAMPERSAD
/ CHRISTELLE SMITH / CHRISTEL STEENKAMP
/ CICILLIA FUMI TSHABALALA / CLARE
KALKWARF / CLARISSA LINDOOR / CLEO
PILLAY / COLLEEN NEBIT (SWART) / CODINE
NUYS / COURTNEY PIETERS / CRYSTAL
KESTEN / CYTHERIA REX / DANEL
ROOSKRANS / DANIELLE SASS / DAPHNE
MAVIS HIGGINS / DAWN BASDEO / DENISE
GAWLER / DENISE SALEM / DENUSHE
WITBOOI / DESIREE MURUGAN / DEVINA
EUROPA / DIANE SAULS / DIANNE ROSE
AYRES / DIMAKATSO JANE NDARALA /
DOMA C PEACOCK (DR) / DOMINIQUE DU
PLOOY / DORNED VAN DER HAAR / DYLAN
NEETHLING / EDNA JANSE VAN VUUREN /
EDWINA HOBBS / EDWINA THOMAS / EILEEN
ALLISTER / ALAINE CONRADIE / ELAINE

VENTER / ELDA JAFTHA / ELEANOR
WYNGAARDT / ELIZABETH JACOMINA /
ELIZE JURIES / ELIZE MEYER / ELIZMA
PIETERSEN / ELMIEN STEYN / ELSIE WOUDA /
ELZONA MAY / EMAAN SOLOMONS / EMIHLE
EMZA MANZIMA / EMMA WALL /
EMMERANCIA ANNA-MARIE ROMAN / ENTLE
KOMISA / ERIKA CROESER / ERNESTINE
MULLER BRAAF / ERNESTINE VAN WYK /
ESBIE KOSTER / ESMERALDA ISAACS /
ESTHER MAGWAZA / EVANGILINE
BROCKMAN / EUREKA HUMAN / FAITH
QWELANE / FATIEMA EBRAHIM / FATIMA
PATEL / FELICIA OKTOBER / FEMIDA WILLIES
/ FEZIKILE KUZWAYO / FEZEKA JORDAN /
KATLEGO PHASHA / TSHEPO PHASHA / FIONA
HARVEY / FRANCIS HAMWIJK CRUYWAGEN /
FRANCIONETTE JANTJIES / FRANZISKA
BLÖCHLIGER / FRIEDA ARENDSE / GABISILE
SHABANE / GABRIELA ALBAN / GAIL
STOKELL / GAIL VAN AS-ROBERTS /
GENOVEVE ASSEGAAI / GEORGIA BLUME /
GERALDINE VIENNA / GERALDINE BLUME /
GILL PACKHAM / GINA VAN DER MERWE /
GIO ARENDSE / GITA SAMGI / GLADYS
HANNA MAKALENI / GLENDA SAMSODIEN /
GLORIA MANYAKO / GOMOLEMO LEGAE /
GRANNY BUYELWA MALILA / ASEMAHLE
MTSORHA / ATHENKOSI ZONDI / GWEN RIST /
GWEN WALL / HANNAH CORNELIUS /
HANNSIE VISSER / HELEN FANAROUKIS /
HELEN JANSE VAN VUUREN / HELEN LOTTER
/ HELGA VAN WYK / HENRIETTA PHILLIPS /

HESTER RAWSTORNE / HESTER WESSELS /
HETTIE BIJKERSMA / HETTIE NIEHAUS /
HETTIE UYS /HILARY VAN ROOYEN / HILDA
UYS / HOPE ZINDE / ILSE BARGE /
IMMACULATE NTHABISEND RAMPAI / INA
VAN DER BERG / INGE LOTZ / IRENE
MATTHEWS / ISABELLA MARIA HENRY /
ISSIE DIPPENAAR / IILZE SCHOOMBIE /
ITUMELENG JULIA TSENASE / JADE BURNS /
JADE PANAYIOTOU / JAN VAN ZYL / JANA
VENTER / JANDY PESTANA / JANE
GOVINDSAMY / RACKELLE GOVINDSAMY /
JANET DELPORT / JANET SCOTT / JANET
VERITY / JANIKA MALLO / JANINE DRENNEN /
JANNINE PHILANDER / JASMINE LEE
PRETORIUS / JAYDE GOVINDASAMY / JEAN
MARK / JEANETTE PETERSON / JENNY KING /
JENORLEE BARNIES / JESSE HESS / JESSICA
WHEELER / JILL FERNANDEZ / JOAN HORN /
JOAN MARK / JO-ANITA SCHULTZ / JODENE
PIETERS / JOHANNA CHARLOTTE
BEANGSTROM / JOCYLIN JOLLY / JODENE
PIETERS / JOEY VAN NIEKERK / JOLANDRE
TOLLI / JOPIE DURIEUX / JOYCE BAARDMAN /
JOYCE DENISE IRWIN / JUDITH
REDELINGHUYS / JULIA FAIRBANKS-SMITH /
JULIETTE DAKADA / JUNE NEFDT / KARABO
MOKOENA / KAREN HORN / KAREN TURNER /
KARIEN BEZUIDENHOUT / KATHY
ALEXANDER / KATHY VAN COPPENHAGEN /
KATRINA JAGERS / KAYDE WILLIAMS /
KAYLA MEYER / KAYLA RAWSTORNE /
KEELYN AMY CLAYTON / KEISHA KORTJIE /

KELLY BAIN / KGAUGELO MOLEFE / KGAUGELO TSHWAE / KHANYISILE NTANGA / KIA FAIRHEAD / KIM LEMINI / KIMEERA RAJBUNSI / KHOLOFELO MORERWA / KUNGAWA MAZEMBI / KHULEKANI SHABALALA / KUTLWANO MASILO / KWANELE FEZILE / LAUREN SLEEP / LAURENCIA ZINHLE MATHEBULA / LATICIA JANSEN / LEAH MARCHANT / LEANOR LAMBERT / LEBO KWABABA / LEBOGANG LEMOLA / LEE-ANN GORDON / LEE-ANN PALMAROZZA / LEE-ANN SCHWARTZ / SHEREE SCHWARTZ / LEIGH MATTHEWS / LEIGHANDRE "BABY LEE" JEGELS / LEKITA MOORE / LERATO MOLOI / LES OLIVIER / LESLIE VAN ZYL / LESEGO RABUTHU / LETTY WAPAD / LIAM NORTJÉ / LIESEL VAN DER LINDE / LIESL BREDENHANN / LIESL NEL / LINDA MATATI / LINDELWA PENI / LINDIWE MANGXINGAZA / LINDOKUHLE VUKAPHI / LINDSAY BOYD / LITHEMBA JAMA / LIYABONA MABISHI / LIZELLE NAUDE / FREDERIKA NAUDE / LORRAINE O'CONNELL / LONDI SHOZI / LORRAINE SHEPHEARD / LORNA SHIBAMBU / LOUISE DE WAAL / LOVEMORE NCUBE / LURESE MEYER / LUISA CRISTIANO / LUMKA PAYIYA / LUNKA MAKASI / LYN RUSH / LYNETTE VOLSCHENK / LYNNE HUME / LYNNE JOHNSON / MAGDA HARINGTON / MAGDELINE MPANA MAHLOKWANE / MAKHOZI MANYAYIZA / MAKHOSAZANA NGCOBO / MAMPHO OLIVE MOTSUMI / MANDY MESIAS / MANENE

CAIRNS / MANUELA PIETROPAOLO / MAPULA
JAQUILINE THEKISO / MARGARET DE GOEDE
/ MARIA ADAMSON / MARIA ARANGIES /
MARIE OSTBO / MARIAN BRUWER /
MARIETJIE MEYER / MARIETJIE VAN RHEEDE
/ MARIKE DE KLERK / MARITZA VAN DER
MERWE / MARLENE COETZER / MARNA
ENGELBRECHT / MARSHAY LOUW /
MARTHELLA STEENKAMP / MARYKA
BEZUIDENHOUT KLEINHANS

R.I.P TO RACIAL INJUSTICE VICTIMS IN THE
U.S.A:

AARON BAILEY/ ABDUL KAMAL / ADAM
ARDETT MADISON / ADAM TRAMMEL /
AHMAUD ARBERY /AKAI GURLEY / ALBERT
DAVIS / ALEXANDER JAMAR MARION /
ALFRED OLANGO / ALLEN DESDUNES /
ALONZO SMITH / ALTERIA WOODS /AMADOU
DIALLO / AMIR BROOKS / ANDRE HORTON /
ANDRE LARONE MURPHY SR. / ANNESON
JOSEPH / ANTHONY ANTONIO FORD /
ANTHONY ASHFORD / ANTHONY BARTLEY /
ANTHONY DWAYNE HARRIS / ANTHONY
HILL / ANTHONY MARCELL GREEN / ANTONE
G. BLACK JR. / ANTONIO GARCIA JR. /
ANTONIO JACKSON / ANTRONIE SCOTT /
ANTWON MICHAEL ROSE II / ANTWUN
SHUMPERT / ARIES CLARK / ALTON
STERLING / ARMANDO FRANK / ARTAGO
DAMON HOWARD / ARTEAIR PORTER /

175

ARTHUR MCAFEE JR. / ARTHUR R. WILLIAMS
/ ARTHUR WALTON JR. / ARVEL DOUGLAS
WILLIAMS / ASKARI ROBERST / ASSHAMS
MANLEY / ATATIANA JEFFERSON /
BALAANTINE MBEGHU / BENNIE BRANCH /
BETTIE JONES / BISHAR HASSAN / BOBBY
GROSS / BOTHAM SHEM JEAN / BRANDON
DEVONE SMITH / BRANDON JONES /
BRENDON GLENN / BREONNA TAYLOR /
BRIAN EASLEY / BRIAN PICKETT / BRIATAY
MCDUFFIE / BYRON WILLIAMS / CALIN
DEVONTE ROQUEMORE / CALVIN REID /
CALVIN TONEY / CAMERON TILLMAN /
CEDRIC STANLEY / CEDRICK CHATMAN /
CHAD ROBERTSON / CHANCE DAVID BAKER /
CHANNARA TOM PHEAP / CHARLES D.
ROUNDTREE JR. / CHARLES DAVID
ROBINSON / CHARLES K. GOODRIDGE /
CHARLEY LEUNDEU KEUNANG / CHARLIN
CHARLIES / CHINEDU VALENTINE OKOBI /
CHRISTIAN COOPER / CHRISTIAN TAYLOR /
CHRISTOPHER ALEXANDER OKAMOTO /
CHRISTOPHER J. DAVIS / CHRISTOPHER
JONES / CHRISTOPHER WADE / CHRISTOPHER
MCCORVEY / CHRISTOPHER WHITFIELD /
CIMARRON LAMAR LAMB / CLIFTON
ARMSTRONG / COREY LEVERT TANNER /
COREY JONES / COREY MOBLEY / CORNELIUS
BROWN / CORTEZ WASHINGTON / CRAIG
DEMPS / CYNTHIA FIELDS / D'ANGELO REYES
STALLWORTH / D'ETTRICK GRIFFIN /
DAINELL SIMMONS / DAJUAH GRAHAM /
DALVIN HOLLINS / DANNY RAY THOMAS /

DANTE PARKER / DARELL RICHARDS /
DARRELL BANKS / DARRELL LAWRENCE
BROWN / DARRIEN NATHANIEL HUNT /
DARRIUS STEWART / DARYLL BLAIR / DASON
PETERS / DAVID ANDRE SCOTT / DAVID
FELIX / DAVID JOSEPH / DEANDRE LLOYD
STARKS / DEAUNDRE PHILLIPS / DEION
FLUDD / DEJUAN GUILLORY / DELRAWN
SMALL / DENNIS GRISBY / DENNIS PLOWDEN
/ DENZEL BROWN / DEOMAIN HAYMAN /
DEQONTRE L. DORSEY / DERAVIS CAINE
ROGERS / DERICCODEVANTE HOLDEN /
DEDVIN HOWELL / DEWBOY LISTER /
DOMINIC HUTSCHINSON / DOMINIQUE
CLAYTON / DOMINIQUE FRANKLIN JR. /
DOMINIQUE SILVA / DONALD IVY / DONNELL
THOMPSON JR. / DUSTIN KEITH GLOVER /
DYZHAWN L. PERKINS / ELIJAH GLAY /
EMANUEL JEAN BAPTISTE / ERIC COURTNEY
HARRIS / ERIC GARNER / ERIC LADALE RICKS
/ ERIC REASON / ERNEST SATTERWHITE /
ERVIN EDWARDS / EUGENE WILLIAMS /
EUREE LEE MARTIN / EZELL FORD / FELIX
KUMI / FLOYD GENE HODGE / FRED
BRADFORD JR. / FREDDIE BLUE / FREDDIE
GRAY / GEORGE FLOYD / GEORGE MANN /
GEORGE ROBINSON / GEORGE V. KING /
GERALDINE TOWNSEND / GREGORY LAWIS
TOWNS JR. / HALLIS KINSEY / HERBERT
GILBERT JR. / HOWARD BOWE JR. / INDIA
KAGER / INDIA M. BEATY / IRETHA LILLY /
ISAIAH LEWIS / JACK LAMAR ROBERSON /
JACOREY CALHOUN / JAMAR CLARK / JAMES

CARNEY III / JAMES LEATHERWOOD / JASON
MOLAND / JEAN PEDRO PIERRE / JEFFREY
RAGLAND / JEMEL ROBERSON / JEREMY
LUKE / JEREMY LETT / JERMAINE MCBEAN /
JEROME KEITH ALLEN / JEROME REID /
JERRY BROWN / JESSE JESUS QUINTON /
JESSICA WILLIAMS / JIMMIE MONTEL
SANDERS / JIMMY ATCHISON / JOHN H.
CRAWFORD III / JOHN T.WILSON III /
JONATHON FERRELL / JONATHON LEE ASUZU
/ JONATHON SANDERS / JORDAN BAKER /
JORDAN EDWARDS / JORDAN MICHAEL
GRIFFIN / JOSHUA TERRELL CRAWFORD /
JOSHUA HARVEY / JR WILLIAMS / JUAN
MARKEE JONES / JUAN MAY / JULIAN
DAWKINS / JULIUS GRAVES / JUNIOR
PROSPER / JUSTIN GRIFFIN / KALDRICK
DONALD / KEARA CROWDER / KEITA O'NEIL /
KEITH CHILDRESS JR. / KEITH HARRISON
MCLEAOD / KENDALL ALEXANDER /
KENDRA DIGGS / KENDRA JAMES /
KENDRICK BROWN / KEOSHIA L. HILL /
KEVIN BAJOIE / KEVIN BRUCE MASON /
KEVIN HICKS / KEVIN HIGGENBOTHAM /
KEVIN LEROY BEASLEY JR. /
KEVINMATTHEWS / KIONTE DESHAUN
SPENCER / KRIS JACKSON / LAMONTEZ
JONES / LANA MORRIS / LARRY EUGENE
JACKSON JR. / LASHANO J. GILBERT /
LAVALL HALL / LAVANTE TREVON BIGGS /
LAVON KING / LAWRENCE HAWKINS / LEROY
BROWNING / LESLIE SAPP III / LEVON LEROY
LOVE / LEVONIA RIGGINS / LIONEL GIBSON /

LORENZO ANTOINE CRUZ / MAHLON
SUMMEROUR / MANSUR BALL-BEY / MARC
BRANDON DAVIS / MARCUS MCVAE /
MARCUS-DAVID PETERS / MARIO CLARK /
MARK ANTHONY BLOCKER / MARK
ROSHAWN ADKINS / MARLON BROWN /
MARLON HORTON / MARLON LEWIS /
MARLON S. WOODSTOCK / MARQUEZ
WARREN / MARQUIS SCOTT / MAURICE
HOLLEY / MICAH ANTHONY KAY / MICHAEL
BROWN / MICHAEL EUGENE WILSON JR. /
MICHALE NOEL / MICHAEL RICARDO MINOR /
MICHAELLORENZO DEAN / MIGUEL ESPINAL
/ MONTEZ DEWAYNE HAMBRIC / MONTRELL
MOSS / MUHAMMAD ABDUL MUHAYMIN /
NAESCHYLUS VINZENT / NANA ADOMAKO /
NATASHA MCKENNA / NATHANIEL PICKETT /
NICHOLAS WALKER / NORMAN COOPER /
OLIVER JARROD GREGOIRE / OLLIE LEE
BROOKS /PATERSON BROWN JR. / PATRICIA
SPIVEY / PAUL GASTON / PETER JOHN / PETER
WILLIAMS GAINES / PHILANDO CASTILE/
PHILLIP WHITE / QUANICE DERRICK HAYES /
QUITINE BARKSDALE / RAMARLEY GRAHAM
/ RASHAUN WASHINGTON / RAUPHAEL
THOMAS / RAYNARD BURTON / RAYSHAUN
COLE / REGINALD WILLIAMS JR. / RICHARD
DAVIS / RICHARD PERKINS JR. / RICKY
DEANGELO HINKLE / RITCHIE LEE HARBISON
/ ROBERT DENTMOND / ROBERT LAWRENCE /
WHITE / RODERICK RONALL TAYLOR /
RONELL FOSTER / RONNIE LEDESMA JR. /
ROSS ANTHONY / ROY RICHARDS / RUMAIN

BRISBON / RUSSELL SMITH / RYAN L. STOKES / RYAN TWYMAN / SABIN JONES / SALVADO ELISWOOD / SAMUEL DUBOSE / SANDRA BLAND / SEAN BELL / SHERIDA DAVIS / SHERMAN EVANS / SPENCER MCCAIN / STEPHEN MURRAY / STEPHON CLARK / STEVEN DAY / TAMIR RICE / TANISHA N. ANDERSON / TASHII S. BROWN / TAWON BOYD / TERRENCE CRUTCHER / TERRANCE CARLTON / TERRANCE MOXLEY / TERRY LAFFITTE / TERRY PRICE / THOMAS LEE ALLEN JR. /THOMAS WILLIAMS / THOMAS YATSKO / TIANO METON / TIARA THOMAS / TOMMY YANCY JR. / TONY TERRELL ROBINSON / TORREY LAMAR ROBINSON / TRAYVON MARTIN / TREON JOHNSON / TRY TA'QUAN PRINGLE SR. / TROY ROBINSON / TYRE KING / TYRONE DAVIS / TYRONE WEST / VERNELL BING JR. /VERNICIA WOODARD / VICTO LOROSA III / VONDERRIT MYERS JR. / WALTER SCOTT / WARREN RAGUDO / WAYNE WHEELER / WENDELL CELESTINE JR. / WILLIAM ALFRED HARVEY III / WILLIAM CHAPMAN / WILLIAM MATTHEW HOLMES / WILLIE JAMES WIALLIAMS /WILLIE LEE BINGHAM JR. / WILLIE NEALL HARDEN / WILLIE SAMS / XAVIER TYRELL JOHNSON / YOLANDA THOMAS / YVETTE SMITH / ZIKARIOUS FINT

SENDING LIGHT AND LOVE TO ALL THOSE ALSO NOT INCLUDED IN THE ABOVE NAMES.

MAY YOU FIND PEACE, JOY, LOVE AND
LIGHT IN YOUR FINAL RESTING PLACE.

Gioya Tuma-Waku is an artist born in Kinshasa, raised in Johannesburg and currently based in Los Angeles. She believes that Art is life and that Art reveals our deepest truths and that we are set free through our creativity. Everyday she aims to move in love + light and as an empath believes that the movement and colliding of energies has the potential to create undeniable beauty.

Website: www.gioyatw.com
Instagram: @gioyatw
@perfectlyimperfectent

Born and raised on the west coast shores of Oakland, California, Chaise Angelo Tait has developed a love for writing. Over the last 5 years it's become his muse, and these poems exemplify the colors created between the lines; a time of challenge, reaction, healing, and finally breakthrough. Taking what works, and leaving the rest is something that has helped him, and will help you create your own universe as you read these. So love yourself and go be Gods!

Chaisetait@gmail.com
Instagram: @chaisemanhattan